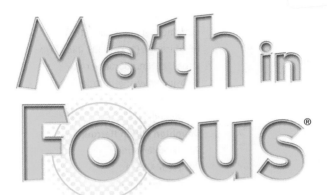

Math in Focus

Singapore Math®
by Marshall Cavendish®

Student Book
Kindergarten Ⓑ
Part 1

Author
Dr. Pamela Sharpe

U.S. Consultants
Andy Clark and Patsy F. Kanter

Marshall Cavendish
Education

Houghton
Mifflin
Harcourt

© 2009 Marshall Cavendish International (Singapore) Private Limited
© 2014 Marshall Cavendish Education Pte Ltd

Published by Marshall Cavendish Education
Times Centre, 1 New Industrial Road, Singapore 536196
Customer Service Hotline: (65) 6213 9688
US Office Tel: (1-914) 332 8888 | Fax: (1-914) 332 8882
E-mail: cs@mceducation.com
Website: www.mceducation.com

Distributed by
Houghton Mifflin Harcourt
222 Berkeley Street
Boston, MA 02116
Tel: 617-351-5000
Website: www.hmheducation.com/mathinfocus

First published 2009

Math in Focus® Kindergarten B Part 1
ISBN 978-0-669-01635-2

Printed in Singapore

15 16 17   1401   21 20 19
4500754264   B C D E

Contents

Contents

Lesson 1 **Solid Shapes**

Match.

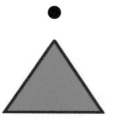

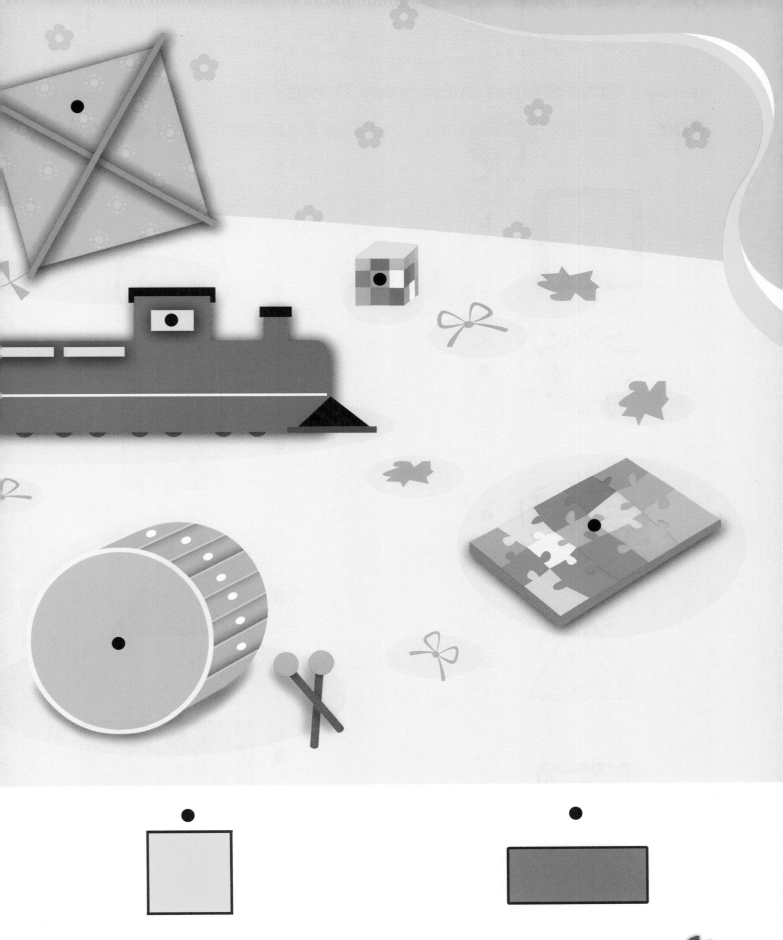

Lesson 2 Solid Shapes in Everyday Things

Pair.

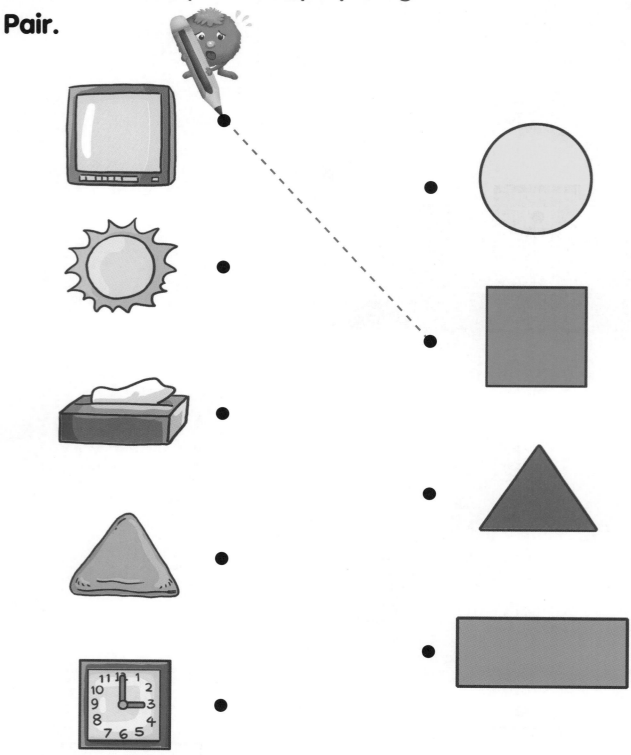

Draw.

Big circle

Small circle

Small square

Big square

Draw.

Small triangle

Big triangle

Big rectangle

Small rectangle

Color the squares red. Color the rectangles green. Color the circles yellow. Color the triangles blue.

Complete the pattern.

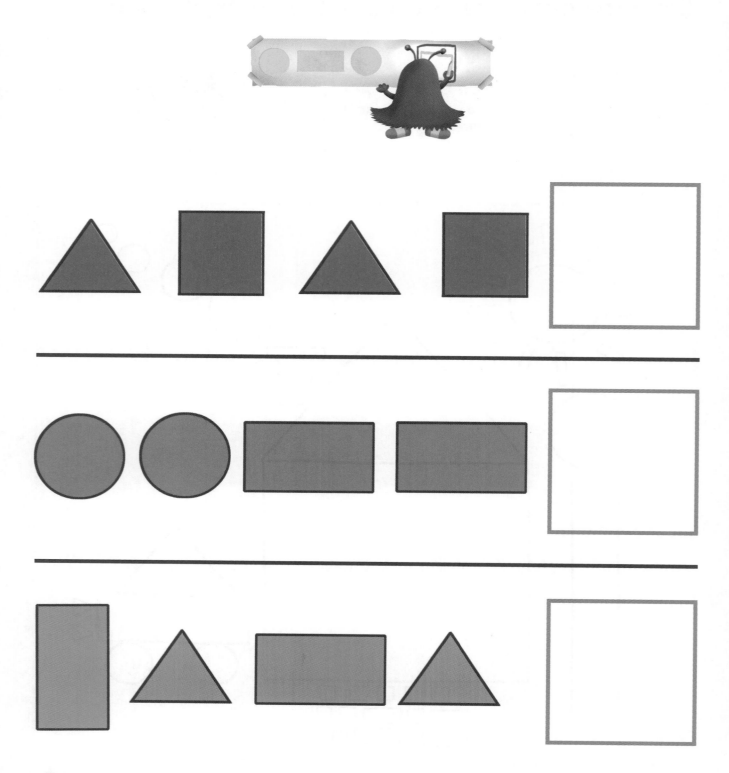

Chapter 8 Counting by 2s and 5s

Lesson 1 Making Pairs

Pair.

Lesson 2 Counting by 2s

Count and write.

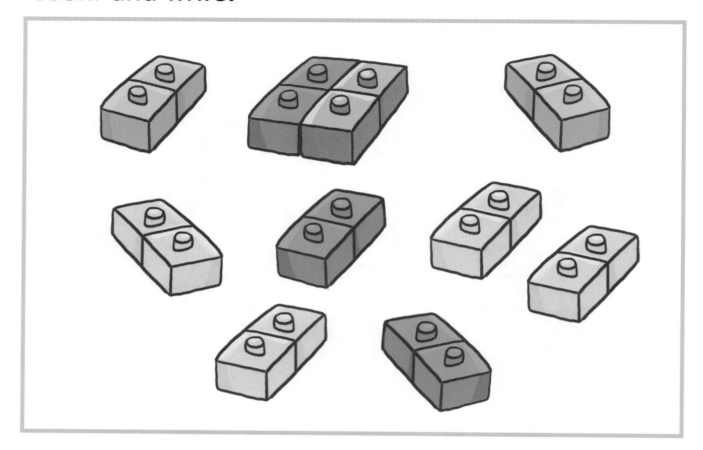

Circle the groups of 5 ants.

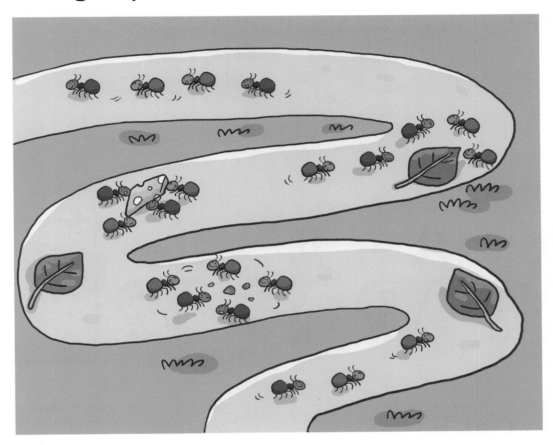

Make the tally.

Lesson 4 Odd and Even Numbers

Count and write. Circle to show if the number is odd or even.

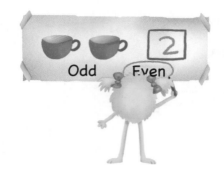

Odd   Even

Odd   Even

Odd   Even

Odd   Even

Odd   Even

Odd   Even

Color the odd numbers red.
Color the even numbers green.

1	2	3	4
5	6	7	8
9	10	11	12
13	14	15	16
17	18	19	20

Number Conservation

Pair.

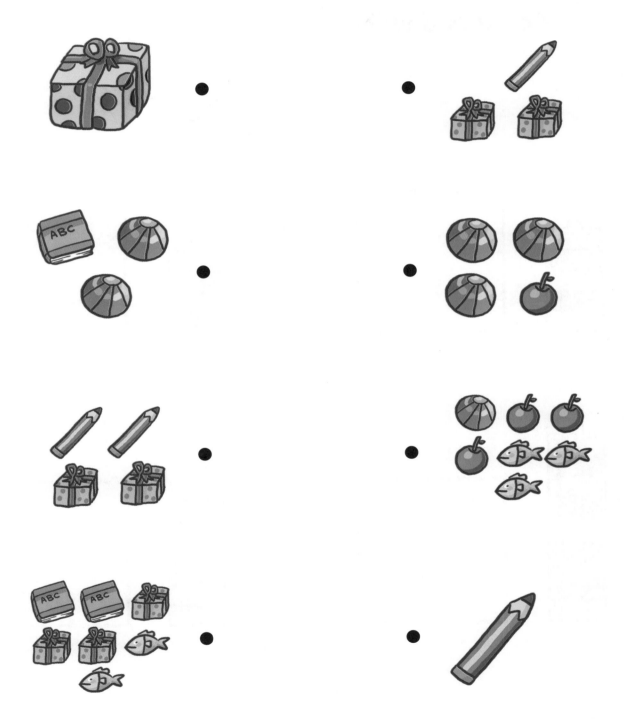

Comparing Sets

Lesson 1 Comparing Sets One-to-One

Count and write.

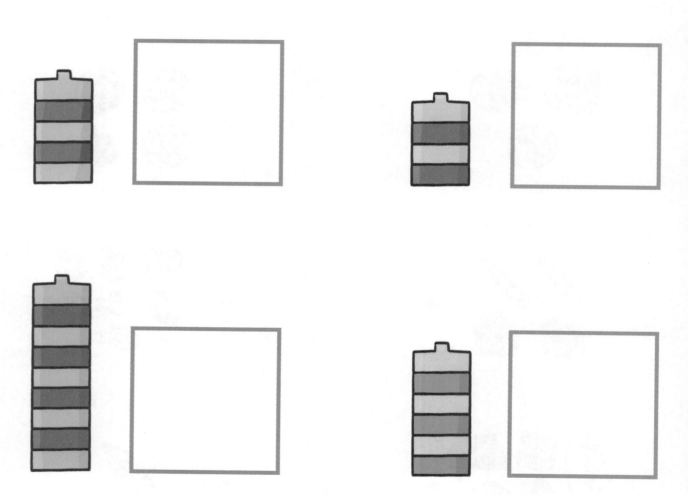

Lesson 2 Number Lines

Count, circle, and write.

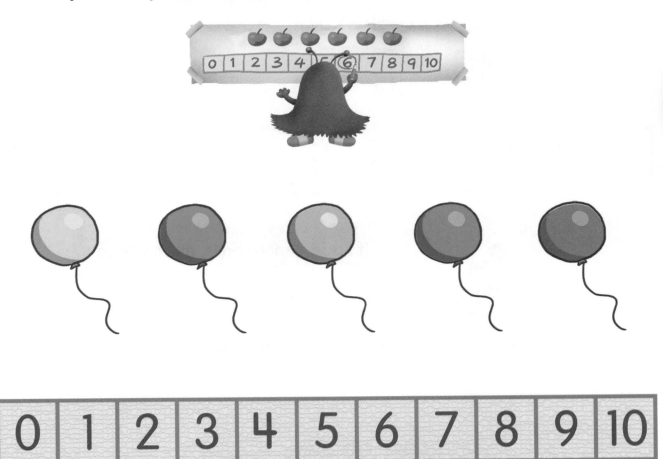

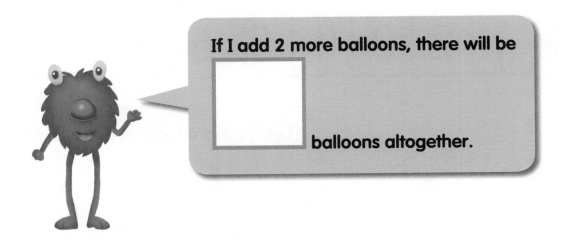

If I add 2 more balloons, there will be

balloons altogether.

Count, circle, and write.

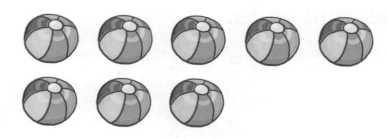

If I add 2 more balls, there will be

☐ balls altogether.

If I add 2 more cups, there will be

☐ cups altogether.

Lesson 3 Fewer and More

Color the extra cubes red.
Count and write how many more.

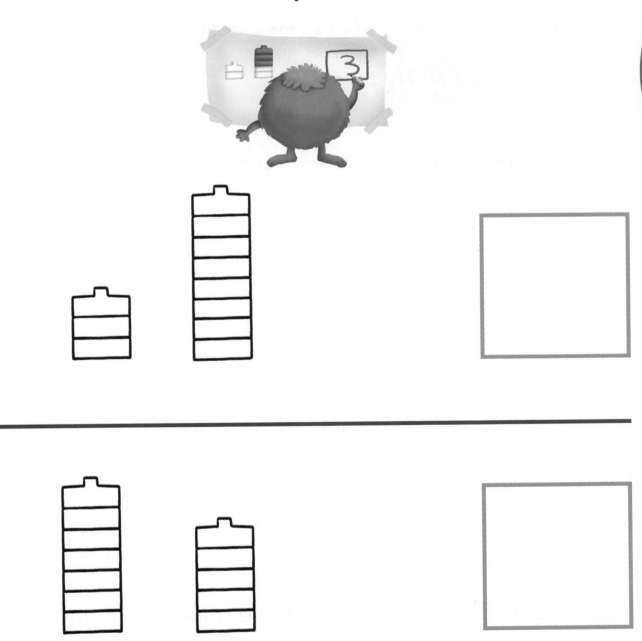

Lesson 4 Comparing Sets to Find the Difference

Draw, count, and write.

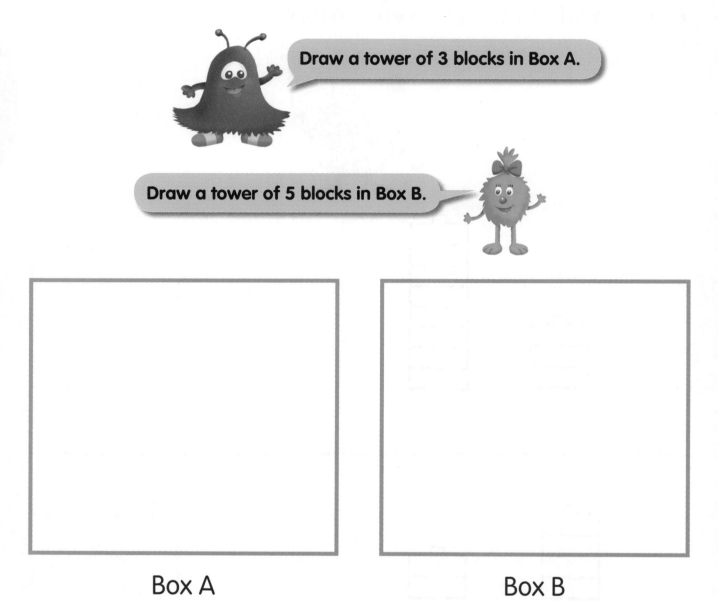

Draw a tower of 3 blocks in Box A.

Draw a tower of 5 blocks in Box B.

Box A

Box B

The tower in Box A has _____ fewer blocks than the

tower in Box B.

Lesson 5 How Many in All?

Count and circle.

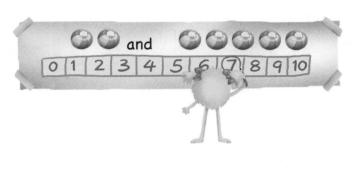

 and

| 0 | 1 | 2 | 3 | 4 | 5 | 6 | 7 | 8 | 9 | 10 |

| 0 | 1 | 2 | 3 | 4 | 5 | 6 | 7 | 8 | 9 | 10 |

Count and circle.

 and

| 0 | 1 | 2 | 3 | 4 | 5 | 6 | 7 | 8 | 9 | 10 |

 and

| 0 | 1 | 2 | 3 | 4 | 5 | 6 | 7 | 8 | 9 | 10 |

 and

| 0 | 1 | 2 | 3 | 4 | 5 | 6 | 7 | 8 | 9 | 10 |

Count and write.

and   is

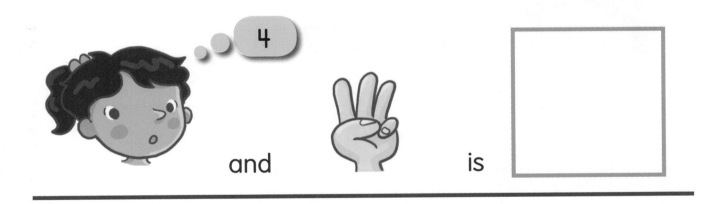

and   is

and   is

Count and write.

and   is

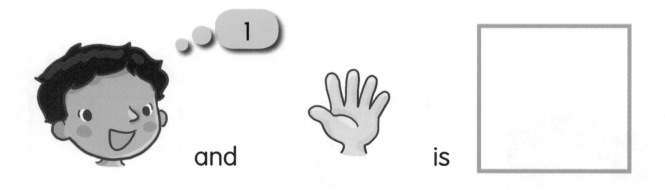

and   is

and   is

Lesson 1 'First', 'Next', and 'Last'

Pair.

first •

•

next •

•

last •

•

Color the frames.

Lesson 2 'First', 'Second', 'Third', and 'Last'

Color.

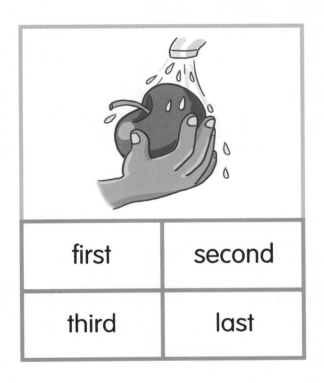

first	second
third	last

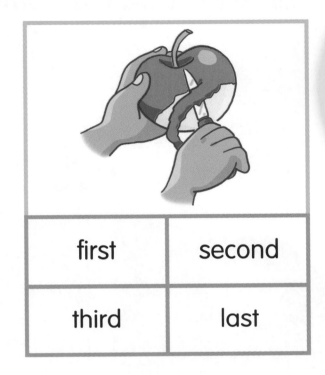

first	second
third	last

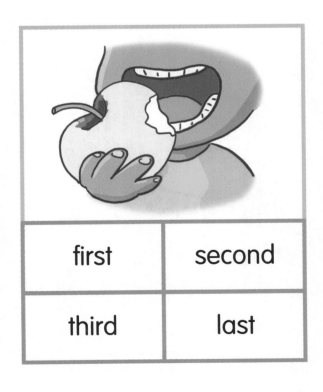

first	second
third	last

first	second
third	last

Color the child that comes before Baby Bear.
Circle the child that comes after Baby Bear.

Pair.

1ˢᵗ choice •

2ⁿᵈ choice •

3ʳᵈ choice •

Chapter 11

Calendar Patterns

Lesson 2 Months of the Year

Make an X on the month before August. Circle the month after February. Color the month between October and December.

1 **January**	2 **February**	3 **March**
4 **April**	5 **May**	6 **June**
7 **July**	8 **August**	9 **September**
10 **October**	11 **November**	12 **December**

Chapter 12 Counting On and Counting Back

Lesson 1 Counting On Using Fingers

How many more to make 10? Count and write.

How many more to make 10? Count and write.

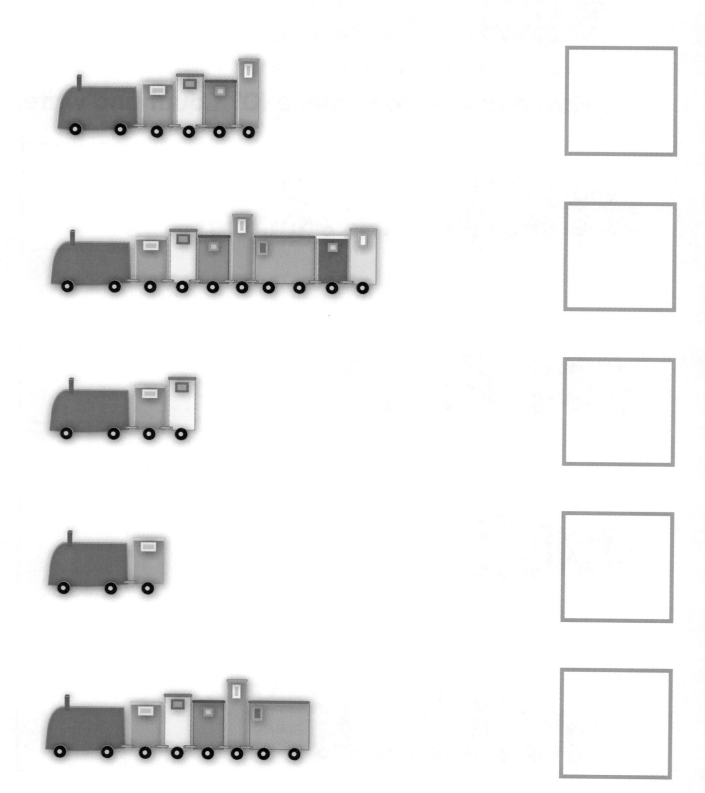

Chapter 13 Patterns

Lesson 1 Repeating Shape Patterns

**The shapes follow a repeating pattern.
Circle the shape that comes next.**

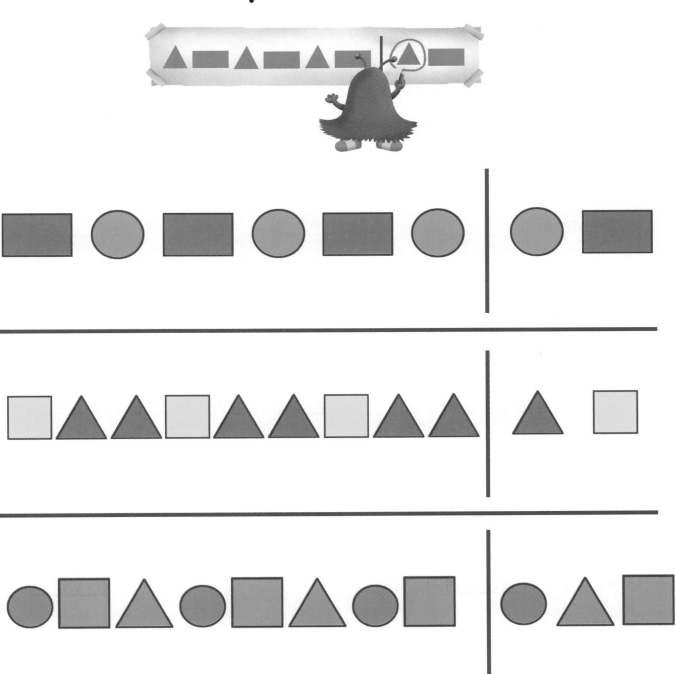

The shapes follow a repeating pattern.
Draw the missing shapes to complete the pattern.

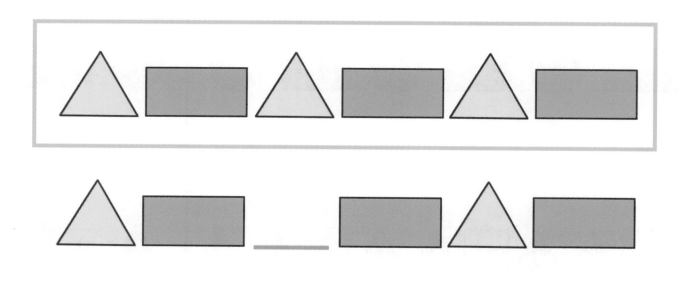

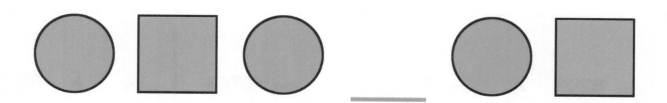

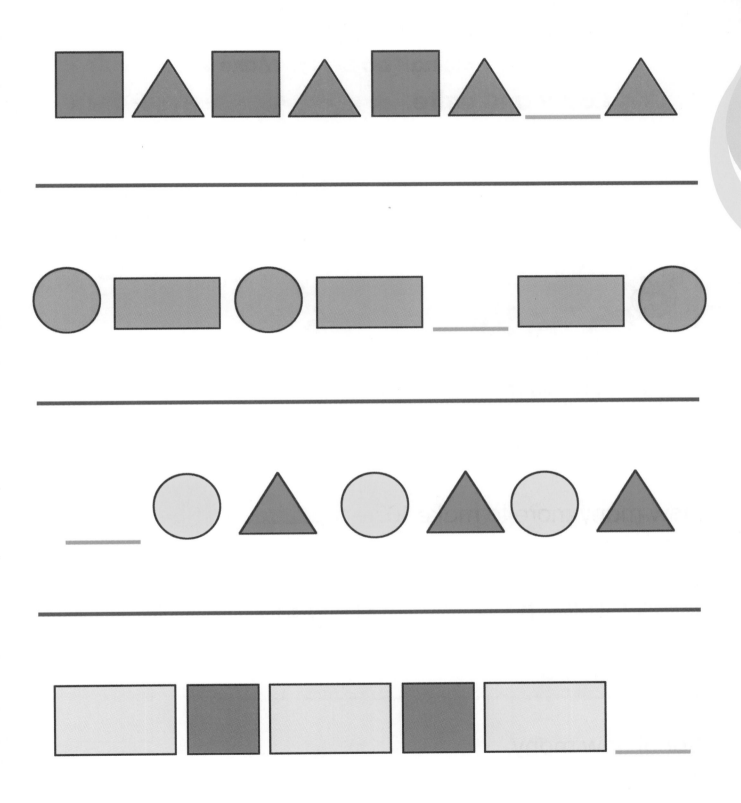

Chapter 14 Counting On to 15

Lesson 1 Combining Two Sets to Make 10

Count and write.

Count how many.
How many more to
make 10?   6
                  4

Count how many.   _____

How many more to make 10?   _____

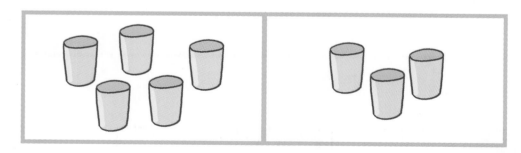

Count how many.   _____

How many more to make 10?   _____

Count how many. _____

How many more to make 10? _____

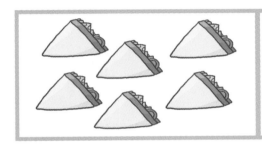 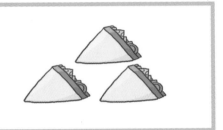

Count how many. _____

How many more to make 10? _____

Count how many. _____

How many more to make 10? _____

Count and trace.

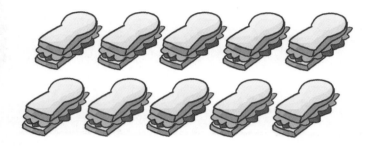 

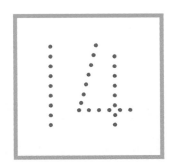

Count and trace.

 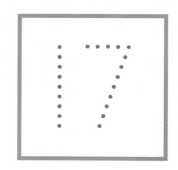

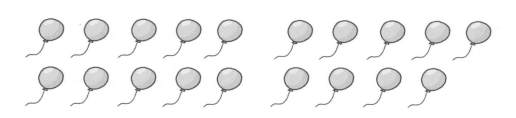 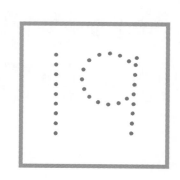

Count and write.

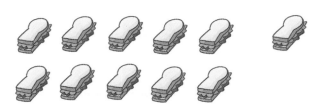

Count and write.

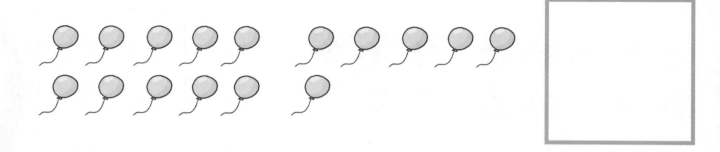

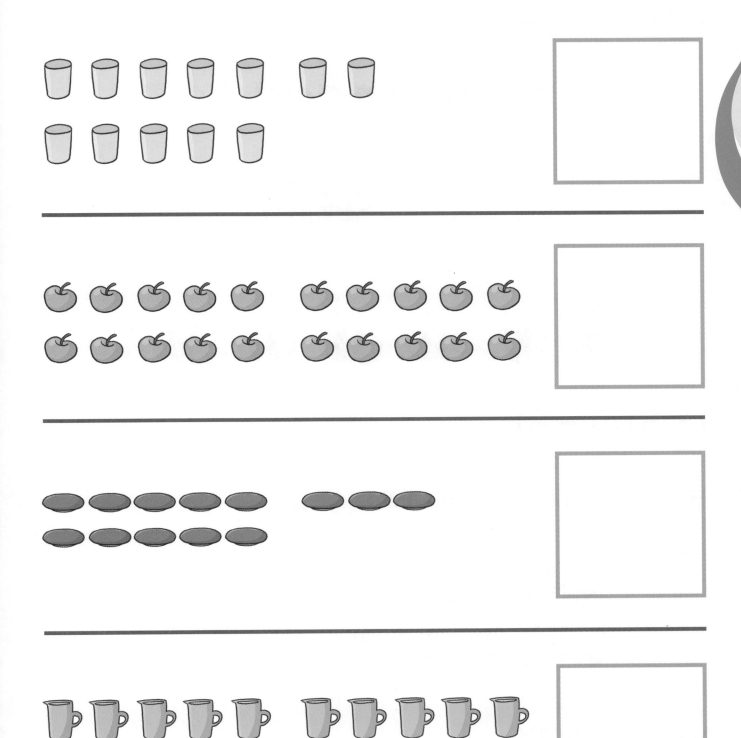

Lesson 3 Counting On

Count and write.

Count how many.
How many more to make 15?

7
8

Count how many. _____

How many more to make 15? _____

Count how many. _____

How many more to make 15? _____

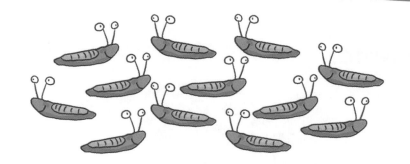

Count how many. _____

How many more to make 15? _____

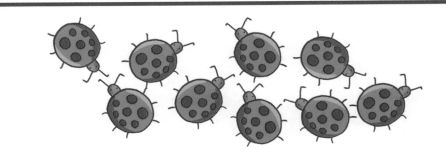

Count how many. _____

How many more to make 15? _____

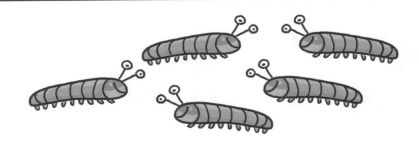

Count how many. _____

How many more to make 15? _____

Count and write.

Count how many.
How many more to
make 15?

$$\frac{9}{6} \over 15$$

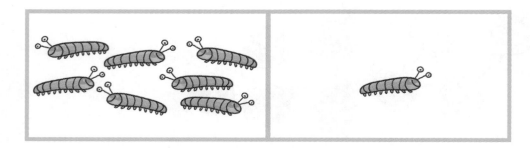

Count how many. _____

How many more to make 15? _____

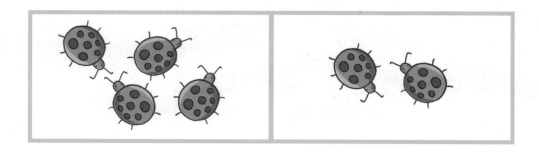

Count how many. _____

How many more to make 15? _____

Count how many. _____

How many more to make 15? _____

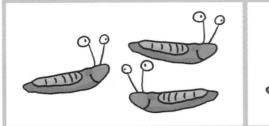

Count how many. _____

How many more to make 15? _____

Count how many. _____

How many more to make 15? _____

Top Cow Productions Inc., presents...

Stjepan Šejić's

Volume 2

Published by Top Cow Productions, Inc.
Los Angeles

Fine Print
Volume 2

Stjepan Šejić
Creator, Artist, and Writer

Ryan Cady
Editor

Logo and design by Šejić • Production by Phil Smith

For Top Cow Productions, Inc.
Marc Silvestri - CEO
Matt Hawkins - President & COO
Elena Salcedo - Vice President of Operations
Phil Smith - Design and Production
Lisa Y. Wu - Marketing Director

Want more info? Check out:
www.topcow.com
for news & exclusive merchandise!

IMAGE COMICS, INC. • **Robert Kirkman**: Chief Operating Officer • **Erik Larsen**: Chief Financial Officer • T
McFarlane: President • **Marc Silvestri**: Chief Executive Officer • **Jim Valentino**: Vice President • **Eric Stephen**
Publisher / Chief Creative Officer • **Nicole Lapalme**: Vice President of Finance • **Leanna Caunter**: Accoun
Analyst • **Sue Korpela**: Accounting & HR Manager • **Lorelei Bunjes**: Vice President of Digital Strategy • **En**
Bautista: Digital Sales Coordinator • **Dirk Wood**: Vice President of International Sales & Licensing • **R**
Brewer: International Sales & Licensing Manager • **Alex Cox**: Director of Direct Market Sales • **Jon Schlaffm**
Specialty Sales Coordinator • **Margot Wood**: Vice President of Book Market Sales • **Chloe Ramos**: Book Ma
& Library Sales Manager • **Kat Salazar**: Vice President of PR & Marketing • **Deanna Phelps**: Marketing De
Manager • **Drew Fitzgerald**: Marketing Content Associate • **Heather Doornink**: Vice President of Production •
Baldessari: Print Manager • **Drew Gill**: Art Director • **Tricia Ramos**: Traffic Manager • **Melissa Gifford**: Con
Manager • **Erika Schnatz**: Senior Production Artist • **Wesley Griffith**: Production Artist • **Rich Fowlks**: Produc
Artist • **IMAGECOMICS.COM**

To find the
comic shop
nearest you, call
1-888-COMICBOO

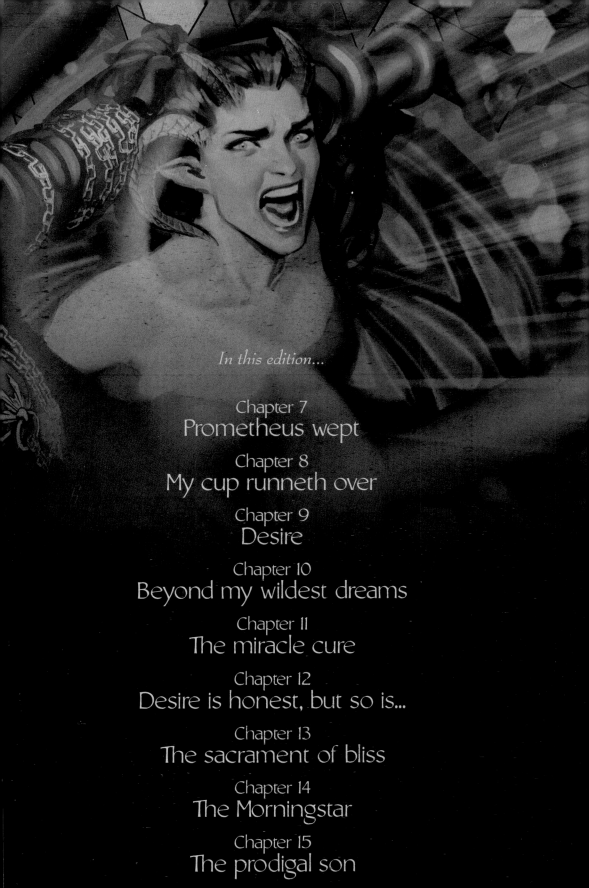

In this edition...

Chapter 7

Prometheus wept

THE FUCKING TEARS...

IT WAS PROBABLY THE LAST MOMENT I WOULD EVER SPEND WITH HIM, AND BETWEEN MY TEARS AND MY GLASSES, I COULD BARELY SEE HIM.

KARMA'S A BITCH, I GUESS...

AFTER ALL THE YEARS I SPENT RUNNING AWAY FROM HIM, NOW THAT I WANTED HIM BACK...THE UNIVERSE ITSELF SEEMED TO CONSPIRE AGAINST ME. CAN'T SAY I DIDN'T *DESERVE IT.*

FOR A BRIEF MOMENT OF CLARITY, HE COMES INTO FOCUS. HIS EYES WORRIED, *DESPERATE*.

FOR A WONDERFUL SECOND, THE RINGING IN MY EARS SUBSIDES, AND HE ANSWERS MY QUESTION. THE LAST QUESTION I WOULD EVER GET TO ASK HIM...

I ------ YOU

...AND HE SETS ME FREE.

suddenly, I feel this tugging sensation. it starts somewhere in my back, between my shoulders and running through my chest. it feels like a chain was pulled -- and with it, a heavy burden finally removed.

BUT EVEN SO...HER PUNISHMENT
WAS TOO CRUEL. THAT LAST MOMENT,
WHEN ALL I DESIRED WAS TO HOLD ON TO
MATTHEW? SHE BOUND MY SOUL TO IT.
I WAS CHAINED BY A DESIRE I COULD NEVER
FULFILL. TORMENTED BY ENDLESS YEARNING
FOR WHAT I COULD NEVER AGAIN HAVE.

LIKE *PROMETHEUS OF OLD*, I WAS
DOOMED TO NEVER FIND PEACE.

AND SO HERE I
AM, SITTING AT
THE SHORES OF
ETERNITY.

PICKING AT OLD MEMORIES,
ENDLESSLY LOOKING
BACK AT MY LIFE.

ALWAYS LOOKING BACK...

...BECAUSE LOOKING
FORWARD...WELL...

...IT SCARES ME.

Chapter 8

My cup runneth over

UNBELIEVABLE!

OLYMPUS REBORN --
OFFICE OF DIVINE
CONTRACTS AND
MORTAL ENGAGEMENT.
TWO HOURS LATER.

NOT A SINGLE
ARBITER WANTS
TO TOUCH THIS
CASE!

FUCKING
BRIMSTONE
AND ASHEN!

THEY
JUST HAD TO
PULL THIS SHIT
DURING MY
SHIFT.

"DO OFFICE
WORK, ALBERT!"

"IT'S LESS
STRESSFUL,
ALBERT!"

"GOOD CHANCES
TO MAKE CONTACTS
FOR ASCENSION,
ALBERT!"

I SHOULD HAVE
BEEN A SEER...

KNOCK
KNOCK!!

ENTER.

MISTRESS
ALARIS. UM...
THERE HAS BEEN
A CALL FOR
ARBITRATION...

SO SEND
AN ARBITER.

USUALLY
WE WOULD,
IT'S JUST...IT'S
A MATTER OF
THIS GOLDEN
CONTRACT
ISSUED BY...

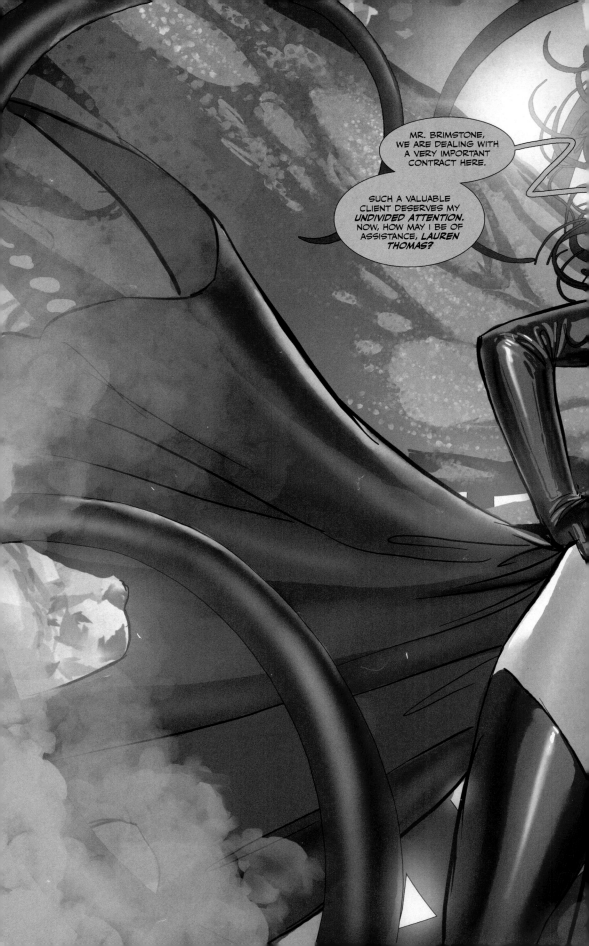

BUT...IF THERE ARE NO CONSEQUENCES FOR *ME,* WHAT'S THE POINT OF A CONTRACT?

OH, THERE *ARE* CONSEQUENCES, BUT THEY ARE OF YOUR OWN MAKING. THE LONGER YOU HOLD ON TO THE SEED, THE STRONGER ITS PERMANENT EFFECTS WILL BE ON YOU.

AS FOR THE CONTRACT, FOR YOU IT IS BUT A LEDGER. A MEMENTO OF YOUR LITTLE ADVENTURE WITH THE DIVINE. FOR US, HOWEVER, IT IS A CLAIM OVER YOUR SPECIFIC SEED. VALUABLE AND UNDISPUTABLE.

WELL... *USUALLY* UNDISPUTABLE.

NOW, I BELIEVE OUR BUSINESS HERE IS SETTLED.

WE WILL LEAVE YOU BE -- FOR THE NIGHT.

WAIT, THEY'RE NOT STAYING?

OH, NO. BUT I ASSURE YOU, YOU WON'T BE NEEDING THEIR COMPANY TONIGHT. THAT SEED WILL KEEP YOU *PLENTY ENTERTAINED.*

AND YET...
I REMEMBER THINKING,
"THIS IS NOT A DREAM."

YOU DON'T *FEEL*
THINGS IN A DREAM.

WHATEVER THIS WAS,
THESE STRANGE ROOTS
WITHIN ME...I COULD
FEEL THEM SINKING INTO
THE FERTILE GROUND
OF MY HEART.

TAKING HOLD --

-- AND I FEEL
SOMETHING ELSE.

COOL.

SMOOTH.

WITH EYES CLOSED, I RUN MY HANDS OVER IT. IT FEELS *LIKE SATIN* TO THE TOUCH.

AND, AS IF EQUALLY CURIOUS, IT TOUCHES ME BACK.

IT CARESSES ME.

EMBRACES ME...

NOW, IF I HAD TO PICK A DEFINITIVE MOMENT WHEN I REALIZED SOMETHING HAD PROFOUNDLY CHANGED, IT WOULD HAVE TO BE THE *BATHTUB EVENT.*

IT STARTED OFF INNOCENTLY ENOUGH.

A SIMPLE DIP TO BRING ME BACK TO REALITY FROM WHATEVER THAT DREAM WAS...

THAT STRANGE DREAM...

EXCITING...

...WONDERFUL...

...DREAM.

THE SENSATIONS STARTED OUT FAMILIAR --

-- IN BOTH THEIR FEELING AND INTENSITY.

BUT THEN...

YOU DON'T *WANT* TO?

OH, UM...

NO, I REALLY, REALLY DO... BUT...UHHH...I THINK SOMETHING IS WRONG WITH ME.

WRONG?

YEAH, I...UM...WELL, I SUPPOSE IT'S OKAY TO TELL *YOU*...

JUST A FEW MINUTES AGO, I...UHHH...

WELL, I STARTED TOUCHING MYSELF, AND... IT GOT *WEIRD!*

LET ME GUESS. SPARKS, SHAKES, MASSIVE ENERGY BURST... AND QUITE A BIT OF NOISE?

WAIT, THAT'S *NORMAL?*

'CAUSE I DON'T WANNA END UP ON SOME FBI LIST FOR CAUSING EARTHQUAKES ANY TIME I WANT TO RELIEVE SOME STRESS!

HAH! NO, DON'T WORRY, IT'S YOUR POST-LINK CONNECTION SETTLING. FROM NOW ON, EVERY EARTHQUAKE YOU FEEL IS GONNA BE WITHIN YOU.

THIS IS WHERE IT GETS FUN. YOU GET TEN TIMES THE PLEASURE, TWENTY TIMES THE INTENSITY, AND A SUCCUBUS AT YOUR BECK AND CALL!

...YOU MADE UP THOSE NUMBERS, DIDN'T YOU?

EH, I MAY HAVE ROUNDED A LITTLE.

THE REST IS TRUE. NOW I CAN FEEL IT WHEN YOU NEED MY SERVICES.

OH?

WHAT ABOUT THE OTHER GUY? THADEUS?

I MEAN... HE'S NOT HERE. MAYBE HE JUST DOESN'T FEEL THE KIND OF CONNECTION TO YOU THAT I DO.

OKAY, FINE... WE HAD TO DECIDE WHICH OF US GOES FIRST, AND I WON!

HEH, WHAT? DID YOU FLIP HIM FOR IT?

SURE, MISS THOMAS. I PICKED BETWEEN HEADS OR TAILS SO THAT YOU CAN GET BOTH.

SO, HOW 'BOUT IT? READY TO GIVE IT A TRY?

HEH...

YEAH... FUCK IT, WHY NOT?

Chapter 10

Beyond my wildest dreams

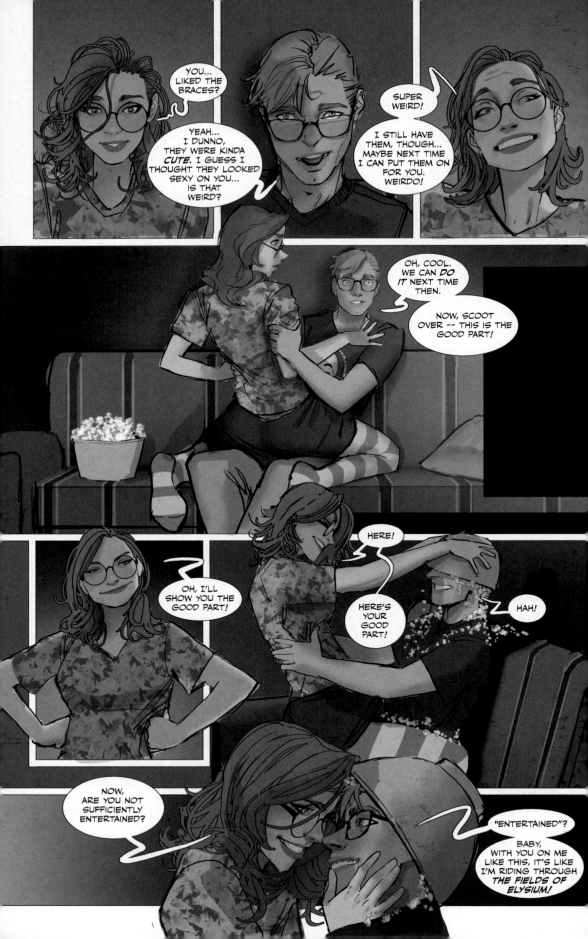

WHAT THE FUCK WAS THAT, THOUGH? I'VE HAD PAINFUL MEMORIES BEFORE, BUT THIS ONE *ACTUALLY HURT.*

I LEGIT THOUGHT IT WAS GOING TO KILL ME.

IT'S THE SEED. FOR SOME REASON, IT CAUGHT TOO MANY *LOVE STRANDS* IN ITS WEAVE.

THE WHAT CAUGHT WHAT NOW?

HUMANS HAVE STRANDS OF DIVINE ENERGIES FLOWING THROUGH THEM.

IN OUR ARRANGEMENT, THE SEED IS SUPPOSED TO BE NURTURED BY DESIRE, BUT HUMANS ARE MESSY.

YOU OFTEN TANGLE UP YOUR FLOWS OF LOVE AND DESIRE.

YOU MAKE IT SOUND LIKE AN EMOTIONAL PINCHED NERVE.

I GUESS THAT'S A FITTING DESCRIPTION.

I SUPPOSE YOUR KIND HAS NO SUCH PROBLEMS...

NOPE.

WE -- UHHHH --

WE DON'T DO LOVE...

BUT BACK TO THE THINGS WE DO ACTUALLY DO!

FEELING GOOD NOW?

YEAH?

ACTUALLY, NOW THAT YOU MENTION IT, I'M FEELING KINDA...

DEVIOUS... AND I SUPPOSE THAT EXPLAINS THE NEED FOR ATHENA'S WHISPERS?

OH, YEAH! THAT STUFF'S GREAT! I CAN READ A BOOK IN AN HOUR!

RIGHT.

SO, WHAT DID YOU LEARN?

WELL, FIRST I HAD TO REMOVE THE ONES THAT WERE ACTUALLY ABOUT FALLING IN LOVE AND THE REST, I SPLIT INTO TWO MAJOR GROUPS.

"GROUPS"?

YEAH, THE ONES ON MY RIGHT ARE ABOUT WOMEN WANTING TO FUCK *ATTRACTIVE, DAMAGED MEN.*

RELATABLE...

...AND THE ONES ON YOUR LEFT?

THESE? THESE ARE ABOUT WOMEN WANTING TO FUCK *ATTRACTIVE, DAMAGED WOMEN.*

WHAT'S THE PHRASE? "COVERING ALL YOUR BASES"?

HEY... I GOTTA WIN THIS FOR US.

AND I CAN'T UNDER-ESTIMATE LELIAH. AFTER ALL, I TAUGHT HER EVERYTHING I KNOW, AND SHE'S BEEN LEARNING EVER SINCE.

WELL THEN, BABE, YOU BETTER HIT THE BOOKS.

MM... NOW, WHERE WAS I?

AH, YES.

"AS THE TREMBLING SUBSIDED AND MY BODY FINALLY RELAXED, I REACHED THE CALM SHORES OF THAT POST-COITAL BLISS.

"AND THERE HE WAS, WAITING FOR ME.

"THE EYES THAT ONCE BURNED WITH PASSION NOW CAST A WARM GAZE UPON ME, AND I KNEW THAT I WAS LOVED."

SIGH... THERE'S THAT FLOWERY NONSENSE AGAIN...

Chapter 11

The miracle cure

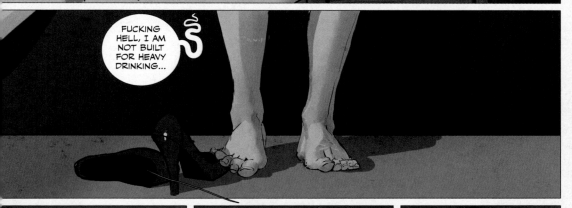

HERE.

NO, WAIT. THIS ONE IS MINE.

THIS ONE IS YOURS. YOU ALMOST LEFT IT AT THE BAR.

OH, THANK GOD!

YOU SAID IT WASN'T A WEDDING RING...

IT'S NOT...JUST A REMINDER OF OLD PAINS... OF A WOMAN WHO RUINED MY LIFE TWICE, AND BOTH TIMES, I WENT THROUGH THE PAIN OF *EXCISING* HER FROM MY HEART.

YOU MAKE HER SOUND LIKE CANCER.

SIGH...

HEY, I'M NOT JUDGING.

SO, WHY DON'T YOU JUST GET RID OF IT?

WHAT?

THROW IT AWAY, SELL IT...*MELT IT,* I DON'T KNOW.

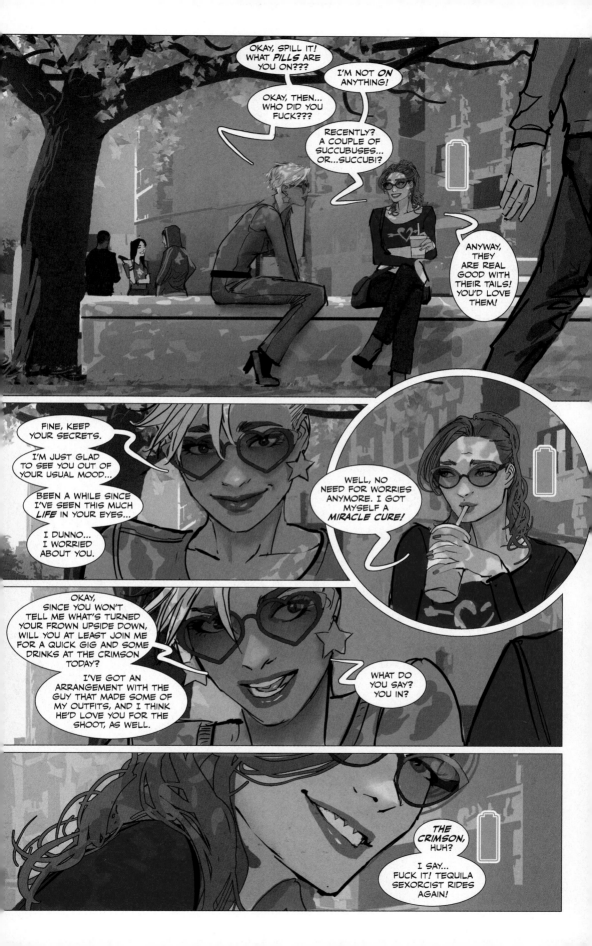

MY MOOD PERSISTED THROUGH THE NIGHT. EVEN THOUGH I WAS NOT A FAN OF LATEX, THE SHOOT WAS A LOT OF FUN.

DUDE NEEDED MODELS, BECAUSE HIRING FRIENDS GAVE HIM PTSD, I GUESS. HE GOT SOME GOOD CATALOGUE IMAGES, AND WE GOT EVEN BETTER PICS FOR OUR SITE. *WIN/WIN.*

AFTER THAT, WE WENT TO THE CRIMSON. I WAS SLIGHTLY DISAPPOINTED THAT *MERRYL* WASN'T THERE, BUT NOT EVEN THAT COULD DAMPEN MY MOOD.

I WAS STILL RUNNING HIGH...DANCING, DRINKING...

...CHEERING ON SAM IN HER PURSUIT TO HOOK UP WITH SOME GIRL AT THE CLUB...

...NOT HEADING HOME UNTIL THE EARLY HOURS OF THE MORNING.

I WAS BUZZING.

THE TRUTH WAS...
I MEANT WHAT
I TOLD SAM.

IT REALLY DID
FEEL LIKE A
MIRACLE CURE.

IT WAS PERFECT...

LELIAH,
IT'S KILLING
ME!!!

WELL, *ALMOST*
PERFECT...

I MEAN, I WASN'T
NAIVE. NO BUZZ
LASTS FOREVER.
EVERY BATTERY RUNS
OUT EVENTUALLY...

BUT THAT WAS FINE,
BECAUSE I HAD NOT ONE, *BUT
TWO* CHARGERS ON STANDBY,
AND IF I PLAYED MY CARDS RIGHT,
I COULD MAKE GREAT USE OF
THEM FOR A LONG TIME!

AND I KNOW THAT MAKES ME
SOUND LIKE A *COLD-HEARTED,
EXPLOITATIVE BITCH*, BUT HERE'S
THE FUNNY PART...

SIGH...

SOON...

SOON, I'LL BE UP HERE, AS WELL...

CLOSE TO THE STARS...

Chapter 12

Desire is honest,
but so is...

OH, I SEE! *THAT'S* WHAT ALL THIS IS ABOUT, ISN'T IT?

YOU JUST WANT LAUREN'S CONTRACT!

"LAUREN." SUCH A LOVELY NAME.

IT IS *AMONG* THE THINGS I DESIRE, YES. BUT I WOULDN'T MIND HAVING YOU BY MY SIDE.

NO!!

CRACKLE

REDBIRD, YOU'RE BEING HYSTERICAL, CALM DOWN AND...

NO! LET GO OF ME!

FWOOOH

WAIT!!!

SIGH...

SO DRAMATIC.

GODREALMS: SHIMMERWOOD.

AAAH!!!!

HUFF

HUFF

WHAT --

OH, FUCK ME, WHAT HAVE I DONE??

I JUST BLEW OFF ALURIA BECAUSE OF THAT BLOODY CONTRACT...

FUCK!

NO, WAIT...

IT WASN'T THE CONTRACT. IT WAS... SOMETHING ELSE.

SOMETHING WRONG...

WHAT'S WRONG?!

BWAH!?

Chapter 13

The sacrament of bliss

BUT IT WAS AS FAR FROM FINE AS IT COULD BE...

BECAUSE THAT WAS WHEN *THE FLASHES* FIRST STARTED...

AH, MISS THOMAS...

...AND I WAS NO LONGER IN HIS OFFICE.

I WAS IN THE *OTHER ONE*.

HER OFFICE.

HER...

AH, MISS THOMAS...

WELCOME TO OUR FAMILY!

AT FIRST, MY BREATH WAS TRAPPED INSIDE MY CHEST.

MY HEART TRIED TO RIP ITS WAY OUT OF ME.

AND THE POUNDING...

...MY OWN PULSE, ECHOING IN MY EARS...

MISS THOMAS?

OH, GOD, ARE YOU OKAY?

CAN I GET YOU SOMETHING? WATER?

NGH--

I -- MMHH -- UH, SORRY!

I GOTTA GO!

THE BATHROOM IS ON THE LEFT!

IN THAT MOMENT, I FEEL A SHIFT. DEEP WITHIN ME, A SEED TAKES HOLD.

I FEEL ITS WARMTH SPREAD...

...AND IT'S SO BEAUTIFUL...

...SO LIFE-AFFIRMING.

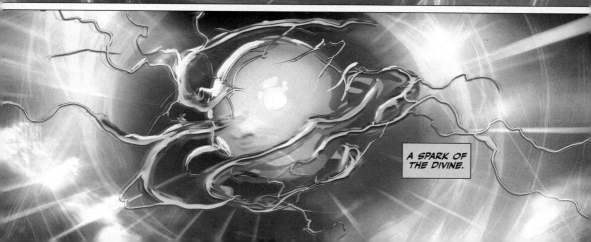

A SPARK OF THE DIVINE.

Chapter 14

The Morningstar

AS YOU SHOULD BE PROUD OF YOURSELVES.

NOW, HAVE YOU ANY QUESTIONS?

Y-YES, SIR, ACTUALLY.

THERE ARE MANY AMBROSIA TREES HERE, BUT *THREE OF THEM* SEEM....

...UHHHH... DIFFERENT?

THOSE ARE THE *ETERNAL SEEDS.*

PRECISELY.

THAT LIGHTENS MY HEART IMMENSELY, BECAUSE HERE I THOUGHT IT MIGHT HAVE SOMETHING TO DO WITH THE FACT THAT THIS CONTRACT WAS DISCOVERED BY *YOUR* PROGENY...BY THE VERY SAME DESCENDANT OF THE MIGHTY ALARIS NAME THAT TRAPPED *MY* SON IN HIS DEAD-END OF A GOLDEN CONTRACT.

BUT I SUPPOSE THAT HAS NOTHING TO DO WITH ANY OF THIS. IT'S ALL JUST A... *MINOR LEGAL HICCUP.*

THAT IS CORRECT.

"THAT IS CORRECT..."

WELL, IT *BETTER* BE. YOU HAD BETTER HOPE THAT ANY LEGALITY ISSUES ARE RESOLVED SOON, AND THE CONTRACT GOES THROUGH... OTHERWISE, THE HIGH CASTE MAY HAVE SOME HICCUPS OF OUR OWN TO DEAL WITH.

AND NOW, THAT SAME SEER OF QUESTIONABLE QUALITY HAS DELIVERED YET ANOTHER GOLDEN CONTRACT, WHEN, IN OUR KIND'S LONG HISTORY, WE HAVE ONLY EVER FULFILLED *THREE?*

EITHER THIS SEER IS THE MOST SPECIAL GODDESS ALIVE, OR SOMEONE HAS BEEN PADDING HER EFFECTIVENESS.

EVERY CONTRACT SHE PROCURED IS VALID AND TRUE. YOU CAN'T TRICK HECATE.

AH, YES, DEAR OLD HECATE. A GOOD FRIEND OF *YOURS* FROM THE OLD DAYS, IS SHE NOT? SHE AND HER PRECIOUS HERMES...

WHAT ARE YOU IMPLYING?

"IMPLYING"? FOR NOW, I'M *IMPLYING* NOTHING.

I AM, HOWEVER, *WARNING* YOU. IF THIS CONTRACT IS NOT RESOLVED, I WILL PERSONALLY PUT TO MOTION THE EXCOMMUNICATION OF YOUR DAUGHTER, MERRYLIA ALARIS, BY REASON OF HER ACTIVITY PRESENTING A CLEAR THREAT TO OUR VERY SURVIVAL.

NOW... *LEAVE ME!*

GRIEF...

...ANGER...

...VINDICTIVENESS...

AND TO THINK...
ALL OF THIS MESS
WAS BECAUSE OF
ME...

Chapter 15

The prodigal son

TO ALL OF
MY PATRONS. THANK YOU!
THIS COMIC COULDN'T
EXIST WITHOUT
YOU!

Wow, you're still here? What can I say but thank you! I hope you liked this second volume in a strange tale of gods and mortals trying to outfuckup each other. Things are obviously only going to get messier from here on out. I mean, we got Bauphette and Lucifer in a straight up Cold War, the outcome of which depends on whether or not Lauren can get her shit together and pick a winner.

This is going to turn into an absolute bloodbath.

And speaking of our contestants, they're off to a great start. Between childish bickering, Leliah's recklessness, and Thad's fussiness, maybe Lauren would be better off with simple assertive confidence of Aluria.

Only time will tell.

Oh, and Bauphette. Everyone's favorite terrifying mom is handling all of this just fine. No red flags here whatsoever. And of course in the center of it is Lauren, a messy human with an even messier life trying to do the healthy thing and drown old pains in new sensations. Puking purple butterflies aside, I think she's doing just great, but then again, having as many regrets and painful memories as she has, who's to blame her...

See you in Book 3, which if you are on my Patreon has started already, so... hey there, that last update, amirite?

-Stjepan

Heureca's design remained relatively unchanged since the first time I drew her. She just...clicked

See you in volume 3!

FINE PRINT

(Or how a divine contract may not be the best cure for a broken heart.)

The Queen and the Woodborn

ANYWAY, NOT EVERYTHING WAS IN SEVENS.

THIS STORY IS ABOUT *THE FOUR*.

SO...

LONG AGO, WHEN MAN WAS YOUNG AND THE GODS SO VERY OLD, THE ALL-SEEING FATHER *SVANTEVID* FELT WEARY, SO AMONG HIS CHILDREN, HE CHOSE FOUR.

FOUR TO GUARD THE GODS' WOODS AND THE WORLD AROUND IT. THEY WERE STRIBOR, SVAROG, PARUN, AND MORANA --

-- BUT THEN, THREE OF THEM LEFT THE FOREST TO LIVE AMONG US!

CYRIL TOLD ME SO!

ARE YOU GOING TO KEEP INTERRUPTING ME, OR WILL YOU LISTEN TO THE TALE?

MPH!

OKAY. YES, THREE CAME AMONG US, AND ONE STAYED TO GUARD THE ANCIENT GODS AS THEY SLUMBER IN THE OLD FOREST.

THE SHIMMERWOOD!

OLD CYRIL HAS BEEN TEACHING YOU A LOT, HUH?

YES! HE SAID THAT SHIMMERWOOD IS THE FOREST OF THE GODS, SPIRITS, AND DEMONS.

AND YOU BEST REMEMBER THAT! THE LAND BEYOND THE GREAT STONE IS THEIRS, AND WE NEVER GO THERE.

LIKE THE OLD FOLK SAY, "STONE-CROSSED IS *WOODBORN* OWED!"

WHO IS WOODBORN?

SHE IS A SCARY OLD THING THAT EATS CURIOUS CHILDREN LIKE YOURSELF.

WAH!

LIKE *BABAROGA?*

SOMETHING LIKE HER.

I'M NOT AFRAID OF BABAROGA!

My Dear Andrew...

Do you still remember the old tales of the Gods?
The three that left the woods, and the one that
stayed behind? I know it all seems so long ago, now...

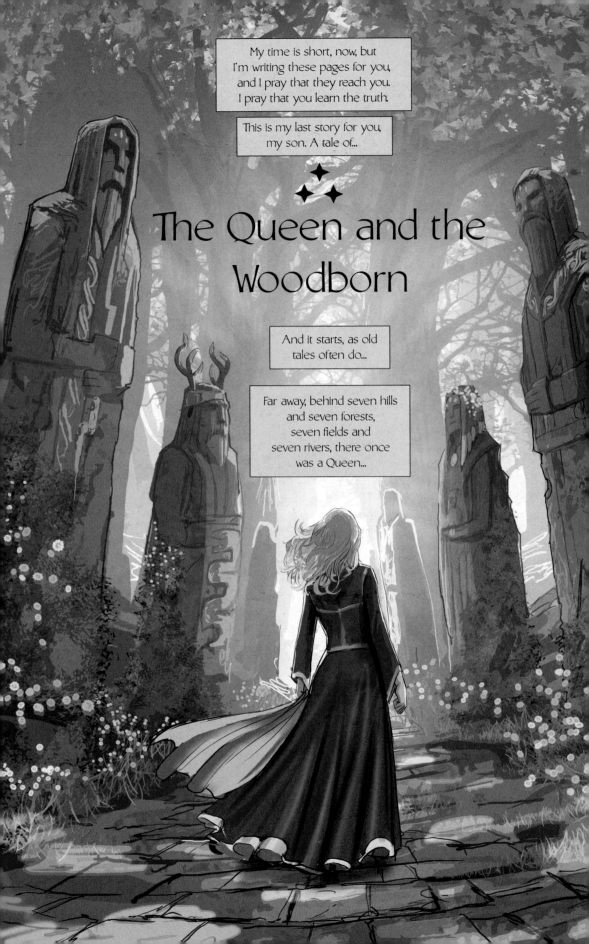

My time is short, now, but I'm writing these pages for you, and I pray that they reach you. I pray that you learn the truth.

This is my last story for you, my son. A tale of...

The Queen and the Woodborn

And it starts, as old tales often do...

Far away, behind seven hills and seven forests, seven fields and seven rivers, there once was a Queen...

I was never a powerful Queen, mind you -- or a Queen of great renown.

In fact, I was once merely the daughter of a lesser nobleman, visiting the kingdom at the border of the Shimmerwood.

Be it due to the whims of my father or the will of the gods, that was the day I met the young king, recently crowned and alone.

The king, your father, took a liking to me...against the advice of the acolytes of the three.

This was not something easily done. One does not go against the voice of Stribor, and yet, the young king did so this one time.

And that one time was enough. That one time, the king stood against all tradition, and, ignoring the acolytes' advice, he picked a foreigner as his queen.

The acolytes never forgot this insult. After all, people in power rarely take kindly to refusal.

Soon, we were married.

It was not a marriage of love. No, never that. Love is the rare privilege of the common folk. There was, however, a certain sense of camaraderie, of duty.

Duty to the gods -- and to the throne. We knew we had to produce an heir, to preserve the legacy of the six generations of guardian kings.

Still, the gods don't bestow their blessings easily...

...and the acolytes, well -- the acolytes whispered ominously, smirking at us. whispering of divine punishments for those that went against their advice.

I won't lie...there were days, my son, when I almost believed them...

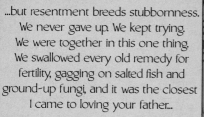

...but resentment breeds stubbornness. We never gave up. We kept trying. We were together in this one thing. We swallowed every old remedy for fertility, gagging on salted fish and ground-up fungi, and it was the closest I came to loving your father...

...because, for every single thing I went through, he was there by my side.

And for those last few months of trying, in the silent hours of the night...I felt that maybe he cared for me, as well...

...and then it happened. The gods blessed us with you.

It was tradition for the old maids of the castle to raise thw future king until the age of twelve, and then he was handed over to the acolytes for six years of pilgrimage and education.

I was never much for tradition.

I wouldn't let you be raised by strangers. Instead, I made my stand -- for twelve years, I would be by your side. For twelve years, I enjoyed my great blessing from the gods...but then...

The years passed. The day came, and they took you away.

This was something beyond my power to stop.

In fact, when it came to power, I would soon learn that I had none.

STOP THIS NONSENSE! THE BOY HAS HIS DUTIES TO TEND TO, AND YOUR DUTY IS DONE!

MY... DUTY?

YES. YOU HAVE RAISED THE BOY.

NOW, IT IS UP TO US TO RAISE A A KING.

YOU MAY REST NOW... YOUR HIGHNESS.

Like i said, people in power don't forget an insult.

And none had more power than Cyril Bogumil. The chosen voice of Stribor, the man who had never forgiven your father for marrying a foreigner against his advice. A man whose resentment was as deep as it was patient. Twelve years, he waited, until you were taken from me -- and then he enacted his punishment.

He did what a voice does best. He spoke, and he whispered of a queen not favored by the gods...a queen best left alone... a queen best forgotten.

And, as if by magic, I grew invisible. It was a curious thing to become a ghost, walking among the living. A memory towards which few, if any, merely nod politely -- without ever truly notifcing you.

I would often seek the company of other memories. Memories of happy days...of the forest, of our trees...memories of you, my son. Unfortunately those memories made my loneliness all the worse.

Oh, yes, my days were lonely. Your father was eventually pushed to find comfort in the company of others -- I never minded that. Like I said, there was never any real love between us. Not enough to merit a sense of resentment.

Still...I would speak lies if I said I didn't, at times, miss him on the other side of my bed.

You see, as the years passed, I developed a habit of waking up at night...and, empowered by solitude, the night's silence grew heavy upon me.

The days were no better.

Lonely weeks slowly gave way to months...

...to changing seasons...

...and to passing years...

...and it was the years that got to me in the end. Years with no word from you, no messages. No letters -- this was what made me face the acolytes for the first time in a long time.

I needed to know.

NOT A *SINGLE LETTER?* HE HAS BEEN STUDYING WITH YOUR BRETHREN FOR *FOUR YEARS* NOW, AND YOU ARE TELLING ME HE IS STILL UNABLE TO READ ANY OF MY LETTERS, UNABLE TO SEND ME ONE IN RETURN???

MY QUEEN, PLEASE! CALM YOURSELF. HE IS A *YOUNG MAN* OF SIXTEEN NOW. YOU MAY HAVE TAUGHT THE CHILD A THING OR TWO, BUT YOUNG MEN ARE MUCH HARDER TO SIT IN FRONT OF SOME BOOK. HE HAS SHOWN PROGRESS, TO BE SURE, BUT HE IS NOWHERE NEAR CAPABLE OF *WRITING ON HIS OWN.*

BUT I ASSURE YOU, IF YOU FIND IT NECESSARY, WE CAN HAVE YOUR LETTERS SENT TO HIS TEACHERS, AND THEY CAN READ THEM FOR HIM, AND EVEN WRITE DOWN HIS REPLY.

WOULD THAT *SATISFY* YOU?

IT...YES. I'M SORRY, IT'S JUST... IT'S BEEN SO LONG.

I UNDERSTAND *COMPLETELY*. IT SEEMS THAT HIS ABSENSE HAS LEFT ITS MARK ON YOUR HEALTH, AS WELL. TROUBLE SLEEPING?

Y-YES, ACTUALLY...

I MAY HAVE SOMETHING TO *REMEDY* THAT.

AFTER ALL, IT WOULDN'T DO FOR THE BOY TO COME HOME TO AN ILL-STRICKEN MOTHER.

There is a tragedy to naivety. It comes from an honest place, a place in one's heart reserved for trust in the kindness of others. And gods know that I was starved for any kind of kindness for a long time. But in the end, naivety is often met by cruelty.

DRINK IT UP NOW, ALL OF IT.

WHAT IS IT?

And that day, I was naive enough to trust an acolyte in Cyril's service. And, after all, why not? However much we disliked each other, I never feared for my safety. "A small perk of the crown," I would think, at times.

MEDICINE, MY QUEEN.

Soon, I would learn how dangerous my naivety was. I would learn that there are potions meant to heal, and there are those meant to harm, and that both often come with a friendly smile.

THERE, NOW.

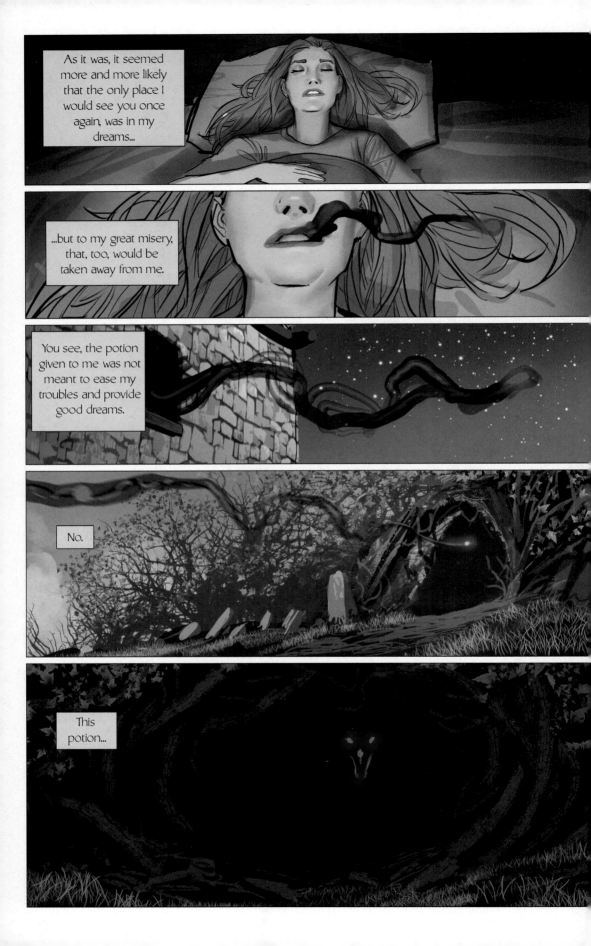

As it was, it seemed more and more likely that the only place I would see you once again, was in my dreams...

...but to my great misery, that, too, would be taken away from me.

You see, the potion given to me was not meant to ease my troubles and provide good dreams.

No.

This potion...

As a small treat, at the end of this story of gods and humans, I offer a preview of another such tale, told in the same universe but long ago. This tale, however, follows the late days of a different group of gods. Deities of the Slavic regions whose stories remain scattered and differ vastly region to region.

This is the tale of the queen and the woodborn.
It is a tale of Danica, the queen of a small, yet important kingdom safeguarding an old forest that many say contains the passage into the realm of the gods. She was never a powerful queen, or even a loved one. She was a stranger in a strange land. Her very presence aggravated the priests of the old gods, as she was not the queen they intended their king to marry. Still, she gave them an heir to the throne. Her duty as a queen was fulfilled in the eyes of the court.

In her own eyes, her duty was to her son. The only person in that cold castle that truly loved her back, until he was taken from her. Sent for education and pilgrimage, and she was left alone.
As years passed, a family ailment took root, and, knowing her years were short, she pushed back against the acolytes of the old gods. This was a mistake she would pay for dearly, as in her naivety she took a medicine from them, thinking it would make her sleep better. Unfortunately for her, it was an essence of nightmare, and it called to its own.

Under the spell of a Mare, she is lured into crossing the great stone, entering the gods' woods, and there she would meet her doom...were it not for the mysterious Woodborn.

A forest witch?
A demon?
Something far greater?
Who can tell, as only those who dare to cross the great stone may find out, but it is a trip without return. Because Stone crossed, is Woodborn owed.

The Top Cow essentials